0901700

JBIOG
Tomli
Lace, William W.

LaDainian Tomlinson

SUPERSTARS
of
PRO FOOTBALL

LaDAINIAN TOMLINSON

William W. Lace

Mason Crest Publishers

Produced by OTTN Publishing in association with
21st Century Publishing and Communications, Inc.

MASON CREST PUBLISHERS INC.
370 Reed Road
Broomall, Pennsylvania 19008
(866) MCP-BOOK (toll free)
www.masoncrest.com

Printed in the United States of America.

First Printing

9 8 7 6 5 4 3 2 1

Library of Congress Cataloging-in-Publication Data

Lace, William W.
   LaDainian Tomlinson / William W. Lace.
      p. cm. — (Superstars of pro football)
   Includes bibliographical references and index.
ISBN-13: 978-1-4222-0546-4 (hardcover) — ISBN-10: 1-4222-0546-0 (hardcover)
ISBN-13: 978-1-4222-0837-3 (pbk.) — ISBN-10: 1-4222-0837-0 (pbk.)
   1. Tomlinson, LaDainian—Juvenile literature. 2. Football players—United States—Biography—Juvenile literature. I. Title.
GV939.T65L33 2008
796.332092—dc22
[B]   2008028191

Publisher's note:
All quotations in this book come from original sources, and contain the spelling and grammatical inconsistencies of the original text.

◀◀ CROSS-CURRENTS ▶▶

In the ebb and flow of the currents of life we are each influenced by many people, places, and events that we directly experience or have learned about. Throughout the chapters of this book you will come across **CROSS-CURRENTS** reference bubbles. These bubbles direct you to a **CROSS-CURRENTS** section in the back of the book that contains fascinating and informative sidebars and related pictures. Go on. ▶▶

02/2009
AB
$ 22.95

◂◂CONTENTS▸▸

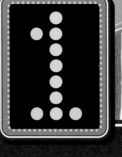

A SEASON TO REMEMBER

On the morning of January 4, 2007, Bill Johnston, the public relations director of the San Diego Chargers, found LaDainian Tomlinson, as usual, in the workout room. Tomlinson was busy lifting weights in his never-ending effort to grow stronger. Johnston was smiling broadly, and Tomlinson thought he knew why. It turned out he was right.

Johnston brought the news that Tomlinson had been voted the Most Valuable Player of the National Football League (NFL) for the 2006 season. The MVP, as it is usually known, is awarded each year to the league's top player, and previous winners

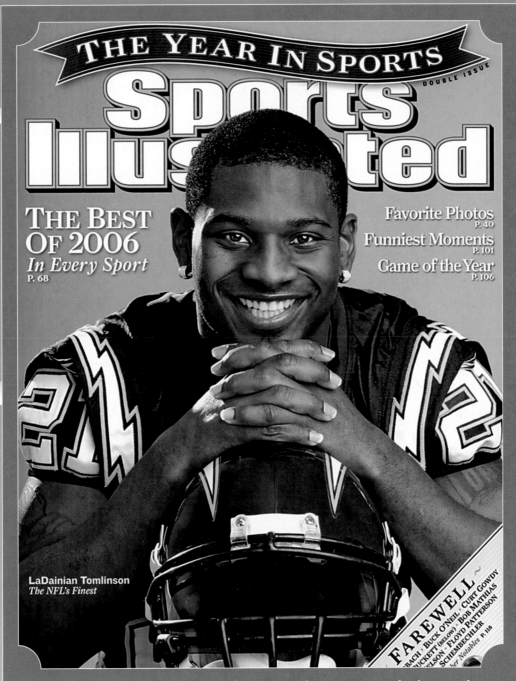

THE YEAR IN SPORTS

DOUBLE ISSUE

Sports Illustrated

THE BEST
OF 2006
In Every Sport
P. 68

Favorite Photos
P. 40

Funniest Moments
P. 101

Game of the Year
P. 106

LaDainian Tomlinson
The NFL's Finest

FAREWELL
...BACH · BUCK O'NEIL · CURT GOWDY
...UCKETT (BELOW) · BOB MATHIAS
...ELSON · FLOYD PATTERSON
SCHEMBECHLER P. 118
...her Notables P. 118

The editors of *Sports Illustrated* came to the same conclusion as the national panel of broadcasters and sportswriters who vote for the NFL's Most Valuable Player: San Diego Chargers running back LaDainian Tomlinson was the best player in the league in 2006.

CROSS-CURRENTS

For some information about the history of pro football's most valuable player awards, read "The MVP Award." Go to page 46. ▶▶

included some of Tomlinson's greatest heroes—running backs such as Jim Brown, Walter Payton, Barry Sanders, and Emmitt Smith. So what was Tomlinson's reaction on learning the news? He just kept on lifting weights.

It was no surprise that LT, as Tomlinson is known to fans and teammates, was not particularly surprised by the award. After all, he had just had one of the greatest regular seasons of any running back in NFL history. His 1,815 yards rushing led the league. He had scored 31 touchdowns for 186 points, both NFL records. He even threw two touchdown passes on **option plays**.

With such statistics put up by LT, voting for the MVP Award had not been expected to be close. It was not. Tomlinson received 44 first-place votes from the 50 writers and broadcasters. Quarterback Drew Brees, a San Diego teammate, was his closest competitor, with four votes.

Team Success

Just as important to Tomlinson as his personal accomplishments were those of his team. The Chargers, who had recently gone eight years (1996–2003) without a winning season, were 14–2 in 2006 and were favored to go on to win the Super Bowl. LT was a big part of that turnaround, but he was quick to give credit to his teammates in an interview on January 4:

> **❝I've had a great season, and obviously before I start talking about myself, there are a lot of other guys of course that have a lot to do with it. . . . All of these guys, [the MVP is] a tribute to them, as well.❞**

The MVP Award was only one of many honors heaped upon Tomlinson as a result of his great season. A month earlier, *Sporting News* magazine had named him its Sportsman of the Year. This award, however, was based as much on LT's off-the-field activities as on his statistics. As Paul Attner wrote in *Sporting News*:

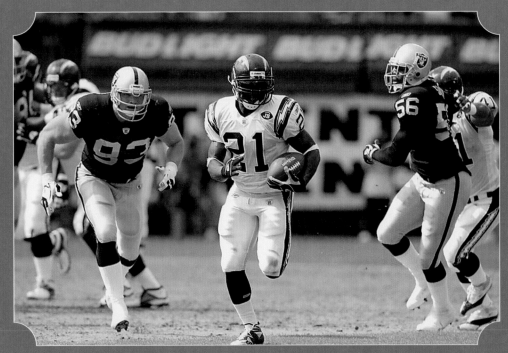

Off to the races: LaDainian Tomlinson blows through the Oakland Raiders' defense during the first game of the 2006 season. LaDainian had a good day, running for 131 yards and scoring a touchdown to help San Diego to a 27–0 victory.

❝ We celebrate his season of history, how he is trampling records of note seemingly on every carry. . . . We celebrate his substance, what he stands for and how he reminds us about what is so good and right about sports and its athletes. **❞**

The article went on to list the many charitable efforts in which LT and his wife, LaTorsha, are involved—football camps for young-sters in San Diego and Texas, thousands of meals for the homeless at Thanksgiving, hundreds of college scholarships, and work with troubled young people through his Touching Lives Foundation.

"Doing Heaven's Work"
Tomlinson's commitment to community service goes far deeper than

that of the typical professional athlete. As Michael Brunker of the San Diego YMCA said in an interview:

> **"LT is always coming to us, asking what he can do. We never have to ask him. That's what separates him from so many other pro athletes. He is an absolute angel doing heaven's work on Earth. He's changing lives."**

One day after being named MVP, Tomlinson added two more awards. He was a unanimous selection to the NFL All-Pro team and was named Offensive Player of the Year by the Associated Press. Once more, the competition was not close. LT received 38 of 50 votes for the best offensive player honor.

LaDainian Tomlinson (left) and New Orleans Saints quarterback Drew Brees display the trophies they received as Walter Payton NFL Man of the Year honorees, February 2, 2007. The two were recognized not only for their achievements on the football field but also for their service to the community.

Chargers officials and players, opponents, and media members joined in praising Tomlinson's talents. **Fullback** Lorenzo Neal, who blocks for Tomlinson on most plays, said in an interview:

> **He's a legend. LT is Superman without the cape. Like Clark Kent before he turns into Superman, LT's a mild-mannered guy. . . . Then, he puts the uniform on and you go, 'My God, this guy's something special!'**

The Walter Payton Award

Yet another award, this one especially meaningful, came to Tomlinson. He and Brees were named the Walter Payton NFL Men of the Year to honor both their football achievements and their public service. LT, who as a youth had followed Payton's career with the Chicago Bears, said he treasured the award because of the influence Payton had had on him growing up.

Finally, in July, the shower of awards ended, but with a flourish. Tomlinson received four Excellence in Sports Performance Yearly Awards, including Male Athlete of the Year, Best NFL Player, Best Record-Breaking Performance, and the Hummer "Like Nothing Else" Award.

Through it all, LT remained modest. He made it clear that the flashy style of some of his fellow athletes was not for him. As he told *Sporting News*:

> **I could do the party thing, but why? It's not worth what could happen. One day [LaTorsha and I are] going to have kids, and I want to set an example for them. I want them to be able to tell folks, 'I want to be just like my dad.'**

This was not something that LaDainian Tomlinson had always been able to say about his own father. Indeed, it had been a long and often very troubled road to stardom from a tiny town in central Texas.

CROSS-CURRENTS

To learn about the NFL running back who was LaDainian Tomlinson's boyhood hero, see page 46. ▶▶

WAITING HIS TURN

For LaDainian Tomlinson, growing up in small-town Texas, fame and wealth were a long way off. Football, however, was always close at hand, awake or asleep. He slept with a ball cradled in his arms as a youngster, and even today, says wife LaTorsha, there is always one at his bedside.

Football was the main link between LaDainian and his father, Oliver. They spent Sunday afternoons watching their beloved Dallas Cowboys on television in their home in Marlin, Texas. The town was just a short distance from Rosebud, where LT had been born on June 23, 1979.

That father-son link would soon be broken. LT's mother, Loreane, and Oliver were divorced, and she moved to the larger city of Waco with six-year-old LaDainian; his older sister,

Londria; and his younger brother, LaVar. Oliver paid visits at first, but they grew less frequent and finally stopped altogether.

LaDainian's love of football, however, was as strong as ever. He entered a youth league in first grade. He ran for a touchdown on his first play.

Starting Out on Defense

Although LaDainian excelled as a running back at every level through junior high school, his first position at Waco University High School

LaDainian Tomlinson has always loved the game of football. As a child growing up in Texas, he slept with a ball in his arms. He began playing organized football in first grade.

was on defense at **linebacker**. Coach Leroy Coleman did not believe in moving younger players ahead of more experienced ones. It was not until his junior year in 1995 that Tomlinson got to play offense, but he started at fullback. His primary task in that position was to block for the **tailback**, a senior.

But before his own senior year began, Tomlinson's mother received an offer for a better job—back in Marlin. If the family moved, LT would have to play his senior year at a new school, one at which he might not be noticed by college recruiters.

Loreane Tomlinson made a difficult decision. She and LaVar moved to Marlin, Londria having married, but LaDainian remained in Waco with a family friend. Loreane made the 30-mile trip to visit her son as often as possible, especially to watch his games.

And what games they were! Finally given a chance to play tailback, Tomlinson became a sensation. He rushed for 2,554 yards and scored 39 touchdowns as University High posted its best record ever. He ran for more than 200 yards seven times, including 216 yards and three touchdowns in the regional finals.

On to College

But even such numbers and a spot on the all-state team failed to attract the top college football powers. Only four universities showed much interest—Baylor, nearby in Waco; Kansas State; the University of Texas at El Paso; and Texas Christian University, about 90 miles north in Fort Worth.

CROSS-CURRENTS

Read "The Recruiting Frenzy" to learn how top high school football players are recruited by major colleges. Go to page 48. ▶▶

Tomlinson wanted to stay close to his family, and Loreane and LaVar had recently moved to Dallas. Since Fort Worth was only 30 miles from Dallas, Tomlinson chose to enter Texas Christian. Besides, TCU, as it is usually called, had his University High jersey number—number 5—available.

TCU had once been a national football power, but it had been in decline for many years. When Tomlinson arrived as a freshman in 1997, the Horned Frogs had enjoyed winning records in just 7 of the last 37 seasons. During LT's freshman year, TCU won only one game.

Waiting Again

Once again, Tomlinson had to wait his turn. As a freshman, he split playing time at tailback with **upperclassman** Basil Mitchell. In his second year, he was moved to fullback. A few games into the season, he protested to head coach Dennis Franchione and was moved back to tailback, but he was still behind Mitchell. Over his first two seasons, he gained 1,255 yards and scored 12 touchdowns. Not bad, but nowhere near what lay ahead.

The 1999 season started on a low note with TCU suffering two losses, but it rebounded in a big way when Tomlinson rushed for 269 yards—third best ever for a running back at TCU—in a win over Arkansas State. Yet the best was still to come as TCU played the University of Texas at El Paso in Fort Worth on November 20.

With the score tied and Tomlinson's rushing the only thing working for the offense, Coach Franchione made a decision:

> **"After three turnovers, I was a little punchy about what to call in the second half. The smart thing to do was to give the ball to No. 5."**

LT carried again and again, and, in the final quarter, he broke away for touchdown runs of 70 and 63 yards on back-to-back carries, pushing his total yards for the game far above 300. The major college single-game record—396 by Tony Sands of Kansas in 1991—was only 13 yards away. Tomlinson broke the record and finally, on his 43rd and last carry of the game, he ran for 7 yards to finish with 406.

He finished the season with 1,923 yards, leading the nation. What meant even more to him was that TCU won only its second conference championship since 1959.

Senior Season

LT's senior season was even better. He gained more than 100 yards in every game, and the Horned Frogs won 10 games for the first time since 1938. Tomlinson again led the nation in rushing, this time with 2,158 yards, and had 22 touchdowns along the way. He finished fourth in voting for the Heisman Trophy, given each year to the nation's top college football player.

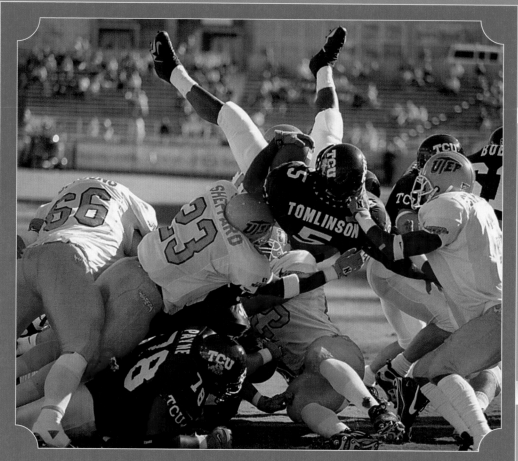

LaDainian Tomlinson topples into the end zone for one of his six touchdowns against the University of Texas at El Paso, November 20, 1999. LaDainian also set an NCAA Division I-A single-game rushing record, running for 406 yards. TCU won the game, 52–24.

It had been a good year in more ways than one. He met a fellow student—and his future wife—named LaTorsha Oakley at a party and eventually asked her out. She was reluctant, fearing LT was just another **self-centered** athlete. On that first date, she later told an interviewer, he took her to a local pancake house:

❝We were there two hours, and I swear he talked about his mom for the entire time. From that moment, I knew he was a sweetheart.❞

Tomlinson had had to prove himself in high school and in college. After his senior year, with the NFL **draft** coming up, he would have to do it again. Despite all his accomplishments, pro scouts had doubts. Sure, he had gained all those yards, some said, but he did so against second-rate competition.

At the Senior Bowl, featuring top college players, he resolved to put on a performance that would silence the doubters. He did, gaining 188 yards. And shortly afterward at the scouting combine, where potential draftees work out for coaches, he far outperformed all other running backs.

CROSS-CURRENTS

If you'd like to learn more about the annual NFL draft, check out "Diamonds in the Rough." Go to page 49. ▶▶

LT's college football career was at an end, but not his college education. He would finish the year short of the credits needed for a degree. He promised his mother, however, that he would earn the degree eventually. It was a promise he was to keep.

The NFL Draft

The number-one draft pick in 2001 belonged to the San Diego Chargers because the team had compiled the worst record in the NFL the year before, at 1–15. The best player available was thought to be Virginia Tech quarterback Michael Vick, but pre-draft contract talks between Vick and the Chargers stalled.

Chargers general manager John Butler was impressed with Vick, but he knew his team needed quantity as well as quality. He let it be known that he would trade the top draft pick in order to get multiple picks, plus perhaps a veteran player. Atlanta, which had the number-five pick, agreed to trade it, plus two more picks and receiver Tim Dwight, for the right to draft Vick.

The Chargers then set their sights on Tomlinson, whom they wanted badly, but they had to hope he still would be available. Arizona, Cleveland, and Cincinnati all were to make selections before San Diego's turn came.

After Vick was taken, Arizona chose Leonard Davis of Texas, Cleveland took Florida's Gerard Warren, and Cincinnati selected Justin Smith of Missouri. A few minutes later, the gamble paid off. LaDainian Tomlinson became a San Diego Charger.

ALL-ROOKIE TO ALL-PRO

As he had done at Texas Christian University, LaDainian Tomlinson would bring fresh success to a team that had seen little except failure in recent years. But while TCU's fortunes turned around in one year, it would be four long seasons, even with LT's heroics, before San Diego would once more be a playoff team.

It even took a while for LT to officially be part of the team. After the draft, in April 2001, contract talks stalled, and it was not until August that an agreement was finally signed. But what a contract it was, especially from Tomlinson's point of view—six years, $38 million, with $10.5 million up front! He celebrated by buying new houses for his mother and sister and a car for himself.

Fans pack Qualcomm Stadium, where the San Diego Chargers play their home games. The Chargers' faithful had little to cheer about before the team drafted LaDainian Tomlinson in 2001. The previous season, San Diego finished with the NFL's worst record, winning only one game.

But football came first. The Chargers' first game was only 18 days away, and Tomlinson had to learn the plays. Most people thought he would have to wait to break into the starting lineup, but LT had waited his turn often enough and would not have to do so again. Offensive coordinator Norv Turner told him that not only would he be the starting running back, but he could expect to carry the football 25 to 30 times, a heavy load for someone who had missed most of training camp.

As it happened, Turner's estimate was on the low side. Tomlinson carried 36 times, gaining 113 yards and scoring two touchdowns as

Rookie LaDainian Tomlinson makes a move in a game against the Arizona Cardinals, November 25, 2001. LT had 75 rushing yards and 72 receiving yards, but San Diego lost the game, 20–17.

San Diego beat Washington 30–3. He confessed to being exhausted after the game, but told a reporter it was no big deal:

> **"I kind of felt like I did in college after a big game, where I had a lot of carries. I was kind of sore, just like I am now. But a lot of people thought I was going to be beat up when actually I feel pretty good."**

Through his first four games, LT amassed 412 yards, 28 more than Terrell Fletcher had the entire previous season in leading the team. Furthermore, the Chargers were on a roll. They won their first three games, including one over Dallas and LT's boyhood hero Emmitt Smith; lost two by a total of seven points; and then won two more to stand at 5–2.

The third game, a 28–14 win over Cincinnati, led some experts around the country to take notice of what LT was doing. He racked up 107 yards on 21 carries and scored three touchdowns. In his review of the game, ESPN's Vinny Cerrato wrote:

> **"Once they get the lead, Tomlinson is the most important guy in the Chargers' offense. . . . [He] missed some of training camp because of a contract impasse, but his success doesn't surprise me. . . . Tomlinson was talented coming out of TCU, and you knew he would do this."**

Playoff Talk

San Diego fans were thrilled and began to talk about a spot in the NFL playoffs. But they spoke too soon. Quarterback Doug Flutie suffered a rash of pass **interceptions**, Tomlinson's performance slowed, and the Chargers lost their last nine games. But despite gaining more than 100 yards in only one game during that stretch, LT still finished with 1,236 yards and became the team's first 1,000-yard rusher since 1994. The rest of the league noticed: he was voted to the All-**Rookie** team and finishing second for Rookie of the Year honors.

The Chargers' 5–11 record was an improvement, but it was not enough to save the job of head coach Mike Riley, who was replaced by Marty Schottenheimer. There was a new look on the field also, as Drew Brees took over at quarterback. Brees knew Tomlinson; the two had played together in a Texas high school all-star game.

A Quick Start

The changes seemed to work, as the Chargers roared off to a 6–1 record in 2002. Tomlinson was a major reason for the team's success. He tied a team record with 217 yards against New England and broke it a few weeks later with 220 against Denver.

But running the ball was not LT's only talent. He had not been used much as a pass receiver in college, and some pro scouts had questioned his ability. But, with 59 catches as a rookie, he'd proved the skeptics wrong. In 2002 he became one of Brees's favorite targets, catching 79 passes for 489 yards.

Although the Chargers again faded over the last half of the season and missed the playoffs with an 8–8 record, LT had a great year. His 1,683 yards rushing was second only to Miami's Ricky Williams, and his combined rushing-receiving total of 2,172 was a Charger record. His feats earned him a second-team All-Pro selection by the *Football Digest* and a spot on the American Football Conference team for the Pro Bowl, an all-star game played each year in Hawaii.

Making a Difference

Meanwhile, LT began to use some of his wealth and influence for the benefit of his hometown of Waco and his adopted city of San Diego. In May 2003 he began the School Is Cool Scholarship fund, helping youth in both cities attend college.

That summer he held the first LaDainian Tomlinson Football Training Camp. It taught football skills to youngsters ages 8 to 18 in San Diego and Waco. He made it clear that his camp was about more than football, as he told a reporter:

> **"Never ever let someone tell you that you can't make it in the sport you're playing. I want these kids to establish team work at a young age."**

Before Tomlinson knew it, it was time for another season, one that he and the Chargers hoped would be better. But while LT would

LaDainian Tomlinson (center) poses with youth at his summer football camp in Waco, Texas, 2003. Each year LaDainian holds one camp in Waco, his boyhood hometown, and one in San Diego, his adopted city.

have a good 2003, his team was not as fortunate. San Diego stumbled badly at the start, losing its first five games. Tomlinson had his troubles, too, recording rushing totals of just 34 and 38 yards in two of those losses.

LT the Passer

There was, however, one outstanding performance. In an **overtime** loss to Oakland, LT rushed for 187 yards and one touchdown and had seven pass receptions. What set the game apart, however, was a play in which LT took a handoff from Brees, headed to his right, then stopped and threw a pass—the first of his NFL career—21 yards back across the field to Brees for a touchdown.

After the game, however, LT refused to celebrate. Any personal accomplishments meant nothing to him unless they were part of a team victory.

The Chargers finally earned that victory at Cleveland, with Tomlinson gaining 200 yards, but it was one of only four wins for the team the entire season. Even so, the season ended on positive notes for both LT and the team. The Chargers beat Oakland, 21–14, and Tomlinson set a team record with 243 yards rushing on 31 carries.

LaDainian Tomlinson makes a leaping, one-handed catch. LT's skills as a receiver were on full display in 2003, when he caught a franchise-record 100 passes.

LT had a respectable 1,645 rushing yards, again second best in the NFL, but his performance as a receiver was even better. His 100 receptions set a Charger record, and he became the first player in league history to rush for 1,000 yards and catch 100 passes in a single season.

But the Chargers' woeful 4–12 record made team officials wonder if Tomlinson would grow frustrated, perhaps playing out his contract and then signing with another team. They decided to make sure that did not happen by signing him to a new contract.

CROSS-CURRENTS

Read "Free Agency" to learn how professional athletes can move to a team that offers a higher salary. Go to page 50. ▶▶

The New Contract

But, as had happened before his rookie year, negotiations faltered between team officials and Tomlinson's agent and were on the verge of falling apart when LT intervened personally. He got a one-on-one meeting with Chargers president Dean Spanos. The two men agreed, and Tomlinson was signed to a six-year, $60-million contract, making him the highest-paid running back in the NFL.

Shortly after signing the contract, Tomlinson said he was confident the Chargers would turn things around. In a news conference, he said:

"I want to be here to make the change. I want to be here when people say what the organization used to be when they were down, and now these guys are up and they are winning. And I want to be part of that group. . . . [Losers] bail out on a team. [They say,] 'So this team is not winning, it's not going anywhere, I got to get out of here.' I've never been that way, so why change now?"

And the Chargers did, indeed, turn things around in 2004—although the season did not look so promising early on. After six games, the team was 3–3 and Tomlinson was averaging 89 yards a game—good, but not what he expected. But San Diego then caught fire, winning 9 of its last 10 games.

CROSS-CURRENTS

LT wanted to continue playing for the Chargers, but a top college player did everything possible to avoid being drafted by San Diego in 2004. For details, see page 50. ▶▶

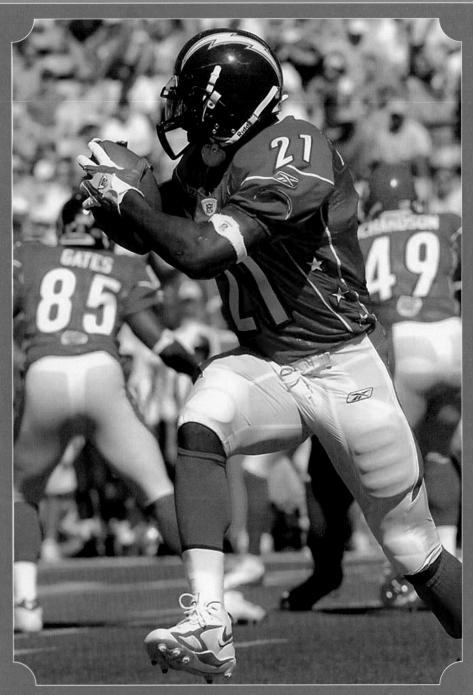

LaDainian Tomlinson carries the ball during the Pro Bowl game at Aloha Stadium, Honolulu, Hawaii, February 13, 2005. LaDainian scored a touchdown in the game, which the AFC won, 38–27.

LT got hot as well. He broke out of a mild slump with 164 yards against Oakland, then averaged more than 100 yards a game the rest of the way. He finished with 1,335 yards despite sitting out the season's final game. His 17 rushing touchdowns were a career best, and he scored in every game except one.

Playoff Disappointment

The Chargers' 12–4 record was their best since 1979 and earned them a spot in the NFL playoffs for the first time since 1995. The playoff game, however, was a bitter disappointment as San Diego lost to the New York Jets in overtime. Tomlinson had a respectable 80 yards rushing, but failed to score a touchdown for only the second time all season.

Still, it had been a good year for LT—good enough to earn him another trip to the Pro Bowl and a first-team selection on the Associated Press All-Pro squad. He was frustrated at the playoff loss, but later, looking forward to the 2005 season, he said it was simply part of his team's growing process:

❝It was our first year in the playoffs in a long time and we had to learn to deal with the emotions of the playoffs. We're more experienced now and we've learned how to channel our energy and how to deal with the peripheral things.❞

A HERO ON AND OFF THE FIELD

Although 2004 had ended in disappointment for Tomlinson, he was eagerly looking forward to 2005, hoping the Chargers could build on their success. It was, however, to be a year of both professional and personal trials. Drawing on his religious faith, he rose above misfortune to have one of the best seasons in NFL history.

Personal tragedy came first. LT and LaTorsha were expecting their first child in April. They had even chosen a name, Mckiah Renee. But, on February 22, LaTorsha miscarried, and the baby was stillborn.

Tomlinson was devastated and in his grief turned to a strong religious core instilled in him by his mother. Still, he said, the loss was difficult to accept:

> **You really think you're in control of your life and then something comes along and slaps you in the face. It takes awhile to get over something like that for the simple fact we had really planned a lot of things already.**

LaDainian Tomlinson is unquestionably one of the best players in the NFL today. Off the field, he is a humble, religious man who is committed to giving back to the community.

Working for Others

The Tomlinsons, denied a child of their own, worked even harder on behalf of others. In the summer of 2005, LT's various projects were expanded and brought under one organization—Tomlinson's Touching Lives Foundation.

LaDainian gives some pointers to aspiring running backs at "Camp LT," 2005. The camp, which youngsters attend for free, is just one of the many charitable and community-oriented programs that LaDainian sponsors through his Touching Lives Foundation.

Football is part of the foundation's focus. At "Camp LT," youngsters get free instruction not only from coaches but also from Tomlinson and other NFL players. Participants also hear about the importance of schoolwork, teamwork, and personal discipline.

Football is also a part of "LT's 21 Club," where 21 youths from the San Diego area are chosen to attend each Charger home game. Some are terminally ill. Others are homeless, in foster homes, or in gang prevention programs. They sit in special seats and receive a free T-shirt and refreshments. Best of all, they get to meet with Tomlinson after the game and, sometimes, go to dinner with him.

CROSS-CURRENTS

To read about the long tradition of NFL players being involved in charitable work, read "A History of Giving." Go to page 52. ▶▶

Two other projects are centered on holidays. "Giving Thanks with LT" provides 1,400 Thanksgiving dinners to needy families throughout the San Diego area. Then, during the Christmas holidays, the foundation gives more than 1,500 toys and videos—many of them handed out personally by Tomlinson—to children in San Diego hospitals.

Educational Efforts

In the education field, the School Is Cool Scholarship program grew out of the days when Tomlinson visited public schools while attending TCU. Hundreds of young people who otherwise might never have attended college have done so through the foundation.

Tomlinson is no mere figurehead in his foundation. He is deeply and personally involved in every activity and makes sure some of his friends are, too. But, as much as he does for others, LT is always on the lookout to do more. He described his views on giving in an interview:

❝We don't put a limit on what we do. I didn't want to be the only one living the good life. I've been blessed and as things come my way, I can keep giving back.❞

Back to Football

Finally, Tomlinson got the chance to put personal grief and community work aside and become immersed in another football season. He admitted it was a welcome relief:

"Every time I'm on the field, even if it's just for a couple hours, I'm enjoying myself just like I was a kid. I think it's a way to get away from things you go through in life.**"**

In 2005, both LT and his team hoped to pick up where they had left off before the playoff loss to the Jets. The Chargers had won 9 of their last 10 regular-season games. Tomlinson had scored a touchdown in each of the final 12 games, and the NFL regular-season record for most **consecutive** games with a TD was 18.

LT scored in each of the Chargers' first two games, but both were losses, and he failed to gain 100 yards in either contest. He and the team rebounded in week 3. San Diego beat the New York Giants, 45–23, as LT gained 192 yards on the ground and scored four touchdowns to raise his consecutive-game TD streak to 15. He then added two TDs against New England and one against Pittsburgh. On October 16 he tied the record in the first quarter against Oakland with a 35-yard pass reception.

Touchdowns Three Ways

Tying the record, however, was not all that LT did. He also scored on a seven-yard run and, late in the second quarter, threw a four-yard TD pass to tight end Justin Peele. That made him the seventh player in NFL history to have rushing, receiving, and passing touchdowns in the same game.

The touchdown streak, however, came to an end the next week in Philadelphia. It was one of the worst games of LT's career. He lost yardage on each of his first four carries and ended up gaining only seven yards on 17 attempts. The closest he came to scoring was in the fourth quarter. With the Chargers at the Eagles' one-yard line, Tomlinson took a handoff from Brees and headed around the left end, only to be hit for no gain by Sheldon Brown.

After the game, the Chargers' linemen were frustrated they had not opened enough holes for Tomlinson to break the record. LT, though, was more cheerful, telling reporters after the game that at least he had made a good run at a new record.

Time Out for TCU

The Chargers had a bye in week 10 of the season, but it still was a busy time for Tomlinson. Saturday, November 13, was "LT Day" at TCU.

San Diego quarterback Drew Brees hands off to LaDainian Tomlinson during the Chargers' matchup against the Indianapolis Colts on December 18, 2005. Although the Colts' defense held LaDainian in check, San Diego won the game, 26–17.

At halftime of the game that night, it was declared that no future Horned Frog would wear the number 5 jersey unless LT himself agreed to it.

He hoped to make another special trip to Fort Worth the next month to receive his diploma, having completed his class work via long distance the previous summer, but he could not fit it into his football schedule. Still, he was proud to have graduated, thus keeping a promise to his mother to do so.

The Chargers recovered from the Philadelphia loss with five straight victories in which LT scored a total of eight more touchdowns. Two losses at the end of the season, however, kept them out of the playoffs.

Tomlinson had struggled through the last four games of the season with broken ribs, but he still managed to pile up 1,462 yards, the sixth-best total in the NFL, and his 20 touchdowns were a Charger record. He went to the Pro Bowl once again and was a *Sporting News* first-team All-Pro selection.

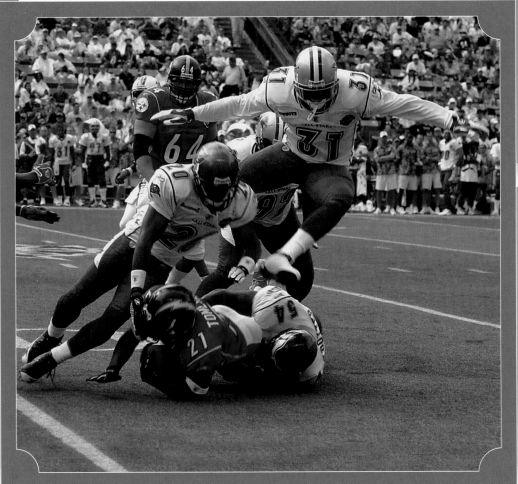

NFC defensive stars gang up on LaDainian Tomlinson in action from the Pro Bowl, February 12, 2006. The 2006 Pro Bowl marked LaDainian's third appearance in the NFL's annual all-star game.

Major Changes in 2006

There would be some major changes for the Chargers before the 2006 season. Quarterback Drew Brees had departed for the New Orleans Saints, and Philip Rivers, the number-one draft choice two years earlier, was the new starter. It was clear that Tomlinson would carry the offensive load, as one fan wrote on a Web site:

> **"The Chargers would be wise to load up on LT, and ride him to victory. Run him, pass to him, let him pass, let him kick. LT is the best player in the NFL."**

In 2006, that might indeed have been the case. He started quickly with 131 rushing yards and a touchdown against Oakland, then hit a stretch of five games of less than 100 yards. However, in one of those games, against San Francisco, he had a career-best four rushing TDs.

In the seventh game of the season, Tomlinson began a rushing and scoring binge. He rang up three touchdowns against St. Louis, three more against Cleveland, and four more at Cincinnati. He had scored 15 touchdowns in the previous five games and had 18 on the season. With seven games to go, it appeared that he might erase the record of 28 TDs set by Shaun Alexander of Seattle the year before.

Alexander's record seemed even more in danger the next week, when LT scored four more times in a victory over Denver. Even his opponents were in awe of his talents; Denver's Gerard Warren compared him to Hall of Fame running back Jim Brown.

CROSS-CURRENTS

For some information on Shaun Alexander, who set the record for touchdowns in 2005, read "Another Record Breaker." Go to page 53. ▶▶

Record Performance

The quest for the record continued with two touchdowns each in victories over Oakland and Buffalo. LT entered the December 10 game against Denver with a total of 26 TDs, 2 short of tying the record. He got the first one in the second quarter with a one-yard plunge off right tackle and the second in the fourth quarter from six yards out.

Then, with about three minutes left, the Broncos fumbled and San Diego recovered. With the Chargers on Denver's seven-yard line,

Historic run: LaDainian Tomlinson turns the corner en route to his record-setting 29th touchdown of the season, December 10, 2006. The seven-yard run came in the fourth quarter of the game, a 48–20 Chargers victory over the Denver Broncos.

Tomlinson went into the huddle. He told his teammates that he planned to score on the next play and wanted everyone to join him in the end zone.

And that is exactly what happened. LT took Rivers's handoff, then swept around the left end and into the history books. His teammates mobbed him in the end zone, lifting him on their shoulders as the San Diego fans chanted "LT! LT!" He continued to share the glory after the game, telling the crowd over the stadium's sound system:

"When we're old and can't play this game anymore, these are the moments we are going to remember. . . . We made history today. There's no better feeling than to share it with the group of guys that's in that locker room.**"**

Reluctant Celebration

A celebration with those teammates was in order, but Tomlinson had to be talked into it by his wife. She joked later that if it had been up to her husband, he would probably have spent the night at home watching a rented movie.

Tomlinson had the record, but he was by no means through for the year. He gained 388 yards and scored two more touchdowns over the final three games to push the record to 31. Furthermore, the Chargers remained hot, ending the year on a 10-game winning streak for a 14–2 record.

Once more, however, there would be disappointment in the playoffs. LT's 123 yards rushing and a fourth-quarter touchdown gave the Chargers a 21–13 lead over New England, but the Patriots rallied behind the passing of Tom Brady to win 24–21.

Tomlinson was clearly upset on the field, but he cooled off afterward. He told reporters that the Chargers had lost to a better team and that he hoped he and the team would learn something from the experience. One season had ended, but he was already looking toward another.

SO CLOSE

LaDainian Tomlinson's preseason goal is exactly the same every year. When reporters ask him, he replies that he has only one goal—for his team to reach the Super Bowl. For two straight years, however, his San Diego Chargers had bowed out in the first round of the playoffs, frustrating players and fans alike. Perhaps 2007 would be different.

All thoughts of football, however, once more had to give way before personal tragedy. On February 23 a truck in which Oliver Tomlinson was riding blew a tire and flipped over on a rural Texas road. He and the driver were killed.

LT and his father had gradually been rebuilding their relationship. After a Texas Christian University game during

After shattering the single-season touchdown record and winning NFL Most Valuable Player honors for 2006, LaDainian Tomlinson signed an endorsement deal with California-based TV manufacturer Vizio, Inc. During football season, however, the only business he cares to focus on is getting the Chargers to the Super Bowl.

LT's junior season, he had looked into the stands and, for the first time, saw Oliver there. A short time later, they had a talk—the first in six years.

Recently, however, Oliver Tomlinson had become increasingly ill. An interviewer once asked LaDainian's mother how the family handled the situation:

"I just told them [her children] to pray for him. They've always sought their dad out. LaDainian's asked him several times to come and stay with him [in San Diego]. He would do whatever it takes, but he refuses to leave."

A New Coach

But, as before with LaTorsha's miscarriage, LT was eventually able to put his grief away and concentrate on football. The 2007 Chargers were loaded with talent. Team ownership, however, thought a coaching change might make a difference. Marty Schottenheimer was fired and replaced by Norv Turner, who had been the Chargers' offensive coordinator during Tomlinson's rookie year.

After an opening-day victory over Chicago, San Diego hit the skids, losing three in a row. Tomlinson, especially, was in a slump. He finally ran for over 100 yards in the fourth game, but he had gained only 130 total rushing yards in the previous three games while scoring only two touchdowns.

LaDainian Tomlinson breaks a run for a big gain against the Kansas City Chiefs, September 30, 2007. In the game, LT snapped out of his early-season slump, rushing for 132 yards on 20 carries. Nevertheless, the Chargers lost, 30–16.

The Chargers bounced back by whipping Denver, 41–3, and the next week evened their record to 3–3 by beating Oakland. The game was a return by Tomlinson to his 2006 form—198 yards rushing and four touchdowns. Teammate Quentin Jammer was impressed:

> **That's vintage LT. He's the best player in the league. He really hadn't got off to a great start, but you know what he can do. You know if you keep chugging at it, eventually he'll kill somebody. He'll probably start killing a lot of people now.**

Wildfires

LT, the Chargers, and everyone in San Diego soon had other things on their minds. On Sunday, October 21—an open date for the Chargers—huge wildfires erupted around the region, burning homes in outlying areas and sending a thick layer of smoke over the city.

Tomlinson's house was in the path of one of the fires. On Monday, he, LaTorsha, and their two dogs hastily relocated elsewhere. Luckily, the house remained untouched.

The Chargers, however, had a home game coming up against Houston, and the thick smoke made practice impossible. On Tuesday, the team flew to Phoenix to practice in the Arizona Cardinals' facility. It was uncertain, though, whether the game would be played in San Diego or elsewhere.

Finally, on Friday, the team got the word that the game could go on as planned in Qualcomm Stadium, which earlier in the week had been used as an evacuee center. Tomlinson later said that just going home had never felt so good.

A Boost from the Governor

The good feeling continued through the game. California governor Arnold Schwarzenegger got the crowd pumped up by cheering for the Chargers after he presided at the opening coin toss. The players took it from there, coasting to a 35–10 win over Houston.

The Chargers could not get any momentum from the win, however, surrendering 28 points in the second half in a loss the next week at Minnesota. Tomlinson's one-yard TD run in the first quarter gave him 107 rushing touchdowns in his career—one more than Jim Brown, one of his heroes—but he was hardly in a mood to celebrate.

San Diego was now 4–4 and needed a big win. It got one the next week as the Chargers knocked off the defending Super Bowl champion, the Indianapolis Colts. Despite being held under 100 rushing yards for the third straight game, Tomlinson got his eighth touchdown of the year.

That step forward, however, was followed by one back—a 24–17 loss at Jacksonville. The Chargers had a chance to win it in the second half, but two drives ended in ways later questioned by the media. First, facing third down and one yard to go in Jaguar territory, Turner elected to call for fullback Lorenzo Neal to carry the ball instead of Tomlinson. Neal was stopped for no gain. Then, facing fourth-and-two on the next possession, LT was called on to pass instead of run. No receiver was open, and he was tackled for a loss.

LT Takes Charge

Writers and broadcasters were not the only ones critical of the play calling. Some of the players were grumbling among themselves, criticizing Turner's handling of the team, especially his use of Tomlinson. The grumbling occasionally went outside the locker room. One player complained to a reporter that there was no commitment to the running game.

Tomlinson decided that something had to be done. The week after the Jacksonville loss, he called a players-only meeting to bring the discontent into the open and deal with it. He admitted sharing some of his teammates' frustration, but then he added, according to a teammate,

❝It's not about the coaches. Between 1 and 4:15 on Sundays, we're the ones who decide our fate. Don't buy into this 'Norv's not a leader' stuff. If we do that we're gonna finish 7–9 and we'll be the ones to suffer.❞

The Team Responds

The Chargers responded in a big way, beating Baltimore the next Sunday to kick off a six-game winning streak to end the regular

LT celebrates a four-yard touchdown run against the Indianapolis Colts. San Diego knocked off the defending Super Bowl champions, 23–21, in the game, played at Qualcomm Stadium on November 11, 2007.

season. Tomlinson was a major part of the drive toward the playoffs. He was held to 77 yards by Baltimore, but in the next four weeks he had games of 177, 146, 116, and 107 yards, scoring seven touchdowns along the way. The 177-yard, two-touchdown performance against Kansas City was the most satisfying for LT because it moved him past Walter Payton on the all-time rushing touchdown list with 111.

The Chargers won the Western Division of the NFL's American Football Conference (AFC), but their 11–5 record was third best overall, behind New England and Indianapolis. That meant they would open the playoffs with a **wild card** game against Tennessee. The Chargers had beaten the Titans earlier in the season, but they had not won a playoff game in 12 years. No one was taking the game for granted.

At first it looked as if the playoff losing streak might last another year. The Chargers could get nothing going in the first half and trailed the Titans 6–0. They pulled ahead in the third quarter, however, and Tomlinson sealed the 17–6 victory with a touchdown in the final period.

Sidelined by Injury

The next victory—against Indianapolis—was just as difficult. In the second quarter, with the score tied 7–7, Tomlinson tried to spin away from a tackler, fell, and was landed on by another tackler. He knew at that point that he had a serious injury.

He tried to keep playing, but he had to head for the sideline after a few plays and stayed there the entire second half. Quarterback Philip Rivers also left with an injury, but backups Darren Sproles and Billy Volek somehow sparked the Chargers to a 28–24 victory and a spot in the next week's AFC championship game in New England.

Speculation was intense as to whether LT would be able to play. His injury had been diagnosed as a hyperextension, or twisting, of his left knee. Although he did not practice during the week, he confidently predicted to reporters that he expected to be 100 percent fit by game time.

CROSS-CURRENTS

To learn more about the championship game in which every NFL player hopes to play, read "The Super Bowl." Go to page 54. ▶▶

LaDainian Tomlinson sweeps to the left during San Diego's wild card game against the Tennessee Titans, January 6, 2008. The Chargers' 17–6 win marked the franchise's first playoff victory in a dozen years.

LaDainian Tomlinson works out during the off-season. As the 2008 football season approached, LT was optimistic about his team's prospects. "I just think we have all the pieces in place," he told an interviewer.

Unable to Play

But it was not to be. LT started the game but had to leave in the first quarter after only two carries for five yards and a one-yard pass reception. LT said later that he reinjured the knee on the first carry and was unable to accelerate as usual:

> **❝If I had kept playing, I would have hurt the team because I didn't have my explosiveness. Sometimes your body tells you it ain't going to happen.❞**

Without Tomlinson, the Chargers lost, 21–12. Any thoughts of a Super Bowl would have to wait. It was yet another disappointment for

LT, made all the more bitter because some media members, fans, and even former players criticized his decision to take himself out of the game. His teammates, however, were quick to defend him, saying that if he had been at all able to help the team, he would have.

The injury was not serious enough to require surgery, and LT was confident that rest and therapy would have him ready to lead the Chargers to another run toward the Super Bowl in 2008. They had come closer each year, and there was a feeling that the next season might see them take the next step.

The Bart Starr Award

But even if LT was not on the field in Arizona for Super Bowl XLII, he was still prominent that day, accepting the annual Bart Starr Award given to the player who best displays outstanding character and leadership in the home, on the field, and in the community. The award was especially meaningful to Tomlinson since it was decided by a vote of his fellow players.

In his emotional acceptance speech, he said that he is often asked where he gets his determination to give so much to others. The answer, he said, is his mother:

CROSS-CURRENTS

For information on some other players who have won the Bart Starr Award for their charitable work, read "All-Starrs." Go to page 55. ▶▶

❝She's the reason. . . . That's the way she was. And that's where it started from—giving back, helping people who are less fortunate and didn't have what I had or what we had as a family.❞

But he also acknowledged his late father, saying that after his father's death, he had been told by a friend that he and Oliver would meet again in heaven and that LT would be asked what he had done with his father's name. With tears in his eyes, he proudly told the Starr Award audience that he is working toward that moment:

❝My last name is Tomlinson. I'm going to do good by it!❞

The MVP Award

LaDainian Tomlinson did not win just one Most Valuable Player (MVP) Award after his record-setting 2006 season—he actually won three separate MVPs.

While the most widely recognized MVP Award is the one given by the Associated Press (AP), voted on by 50 writers and broadcasters, similar honors are bestowed by the Pro Football Writers of America and by the Newspaper Enterprise Association (NEA). There once was a fourth, but the awarding organization, United Press International, discontinued it in 1969.

The winning choice is often an obvious one. In the 33 years since the newest of the three—the one voted on by the Pro Football Writers Association—there have been unanimous choices 20 times. Only once during that period did all three selections differ. That occurred in 1990, when Joe Montana of San Francisco won the AP award, Randall Cunningham of Philadelphia won the Pro Football Writers award, and Warren Moon of Houston won the NEA award.

Numerous players have been named MVP more than once, but only four—Brett Favre of Green Bay, Jim Brown of Cleveland, Johnny Unitas of Baltimore, and Earl Campbell of Houston—have been honored three times. Although every player is eligible, the awards almost always go to quarterbacks or running backs. Of the 34 players named MVP since 1975, only three have not played either of these positions. (Go back to page 6.) ◀◀

In Payton's Footsteps

Of the many honors that came LaDainian Tomlinson's way after his record-breaking 2006 season, perhaps the most meaningful was the Walter Payton Man of the Year Award he shared with former teammate Drew Brees. LT told an interviewer:

> **"**Walter Payton was the reason why I wanted to play football. I remember as a little kid, I was 5 years old, seeing him play and from that point on I told my mother that I wanted to be a football player.**"**

There are, indeed, many parallels between Tomlinson's career and that of the late Chicago Bears running back. Payton also was bypassed by the major college football powers, playing at all-black Jackson State in his native Mississippi. Like LT, he finished fourth in Heisman Trophy voting. He was, like Tomlinson, a high first-round draft choice. Likewise, he helped to turn around a team that had not had a winning season in many years.

Payton's Records

Payton was also a record breaker. In 1984 he overtook Jim Brown as the all-time rusher in NFL history. He finished his career with 16,726 yards—a mark that stood until 2002, when it was broken by Emmitt Smith of the Dallas Cowboys.

Payton also received the same kind of honors that Tomlinson would later win. He was the NFL's Most Valuable Player twice and the Offensive Player of the Year twice, and he was named to the All-Pro team seven times. He won the Man of the Year Award in 1977—22 years before it was renamed in his honor.

Active in Community

Like LT, Payton was an active part of his community. Many of his efforts were the same as those of LT—scholarships, meals distributed at holidays, and programs aimed at underprivileged and at-risk youth. Each year hundreds of Chicago children still receive school supplies from the foundation that Payton established.

Payton retired after the 1987 season, but he never stopped working to benefit others. Early in 1999 he revealed that he had liver cancer, and he died later in the year. He was only 45 years old.

Tomlinson looks up to Payton so much that, two days after surpassing Payton in career rushing touchdowns, he wore a Chicago jersey with Payton's number, 34. He told an interviewer:

> **"**I learned [from watching Payton] what character's all about, I think, even from afar. I learned how to be humble. I think I also learned how to compete the right way.**"**

(Go back to page 9.)

Hall of Fame running back Walter Payton, who played 13 seasons for the Chicago Bears, won acclaim for his heroics on the football field as well as his humanitarian work off the field.

The Recruiting Frenzy

For the die-hard college football fan, the most exciting time of the year is not necessarily the start of the season or the finale of bowl games. Instead, it is early February, when high school players across the nation decide to which colleges they will take their talents.

The most talented athletes will have been getting letters and phone calls since their freshman years. The pace quickens by the time they are seniors, sometimes even juniors, at which point the best-known coaches in the country will visit their homes and they will be asked, in turn, to visit the colleges.

On these visits, recruits will be shown the luxurious locker room, the snazzy athletic dorm, and the state-of-the-art training facilities. The pressure on young athletes has become so intense that, in recent years, more of the best players commit to a college as juniors rather than as seniors, although they cannot sign a formal letter of intent until February of their senior year.

LT the "Athlete"

LaDainian Tomlinson faced no such pressure in February 1997. He was not listed among the top 100 high school players in the country and, indeed, was not listed among the top running backs in Texas. He was on a top 100 list of Texas players, but as an "athlete." This meant that coaches were not sure which position he was best suited to play.

His first choice would have been the University of Texas, but the Longhorns were not interested. Years later he described his frustration:

> **"**I would have loved to represent Texas by going to the ultimate school, which is the University of Texas. But they didn't take a look at me. . . . All these schools were just like I was a second-tier guy.**"**

Other Stars

Although Tomlinson appears, looking back, to have been the best player coming out of high school in 1997, there were plenty of other stars. Fellow Texans Leonard Davis and Andre Gourde have both been Pro Bowlers for the Dallas Cowboys. Quentin Jammer and Chris Chambers are among LT's teammates at San Diego.

Other members of the 1997 recruiting class who went on to NFL careers include Shaun Rogers of Cleveland, Texas Christian University teammate Matt Schobel of Philadelphia, Kyle Bosch and Jamal Lewis of Tennessee, Jason Glenn of Minnesota, Andre Carter of Washington, and Fred Booker and Drew Brees of New Orleans.

(Go back to page 12.) ◀◀

Diamonds in the Rough

Each year the National Football League (NFL) conducts what is officially termed a *player selection meeting*, commonly called the draft. NFL teams pick the college players they hope will turn out to be future stars. Teams with the worst records get to pick first.

In the league's early years, teams often did not know much about the players they drafted, depending on word of mouth or phone calls to sportswriters or college coaches. Scouting, however, has become a science. Enormous files are maintained on prospects. Would-be draftees are weighed, measured, timed, and even given intelligence and psychological tests.

Most of the time, this homework pays off. A recent study of All-Pro players over the last five years showed that half were drafted in the first round and 83 percent in the first three rounds.

Occasionally, however, players have slipped through the cracks, going unnoticed only to become NFL stars later. Pro Bowl tight end Antonio Gates, LaDainian Tomlinson's San Diego teammate, is such a case, having played basketball in college instead of football. Another Charger Pro Bowler, guard Kris Dielman, also was overlooked.

Several players have been skipped over in the draft and have gone on to places in the Pro Football Hall of Fame. Examples include quarterback Warren Moon, and defensive backs Willie Brown and Dick "Night Train" Lane.

(Go back to page 15.) ◀◀

A pro prospect is timed in the 40-yard dash at the NFL's 2008 scouting combine. Each year, before the NFL draft, top college players are invited to the combine, where their speed, strength, and skills are tested.

Free Agency

The Chargers signed LaDainian Tomlinson to a new contract in 2004 because they feared that he might play out the remaining years on his original contract and then jump to another team. He would have been able to do so under a system known as free agency.

For most of the history of professional sports in the United States, such a move would have been impossible. Every player's contract included the "reserve clause." This meant that the player was bound to his original team even when a contract expired. If a new contract could not be agreed upon, the player had no other option.

In 1957 the U.S. Supreme Court ruled that the reserve clause did not apply to the National Football League (NFL). But the ability of players to move from one team to another was restricted by the "Rozelle Rule." NFL commissioner Pete Rozelle decreed that any team signing a player from another team had to pay back the original team somehow—in cash, draft choices, or another player. Teams feared they would lose out in such deals, so few players were affected.

The NFL Players Association twice went on strike, in an attempt to win true free agency of the kind that had existed in baseball since 1975. Not until 1992, however, did players win free agency in exchange for allowing the league to introduce a limit, or "cap," on teams' salaries.

(Go back to page 23.)

The Eli Manning Affair

The San Diego Chargers' 4–12 record in 2003 tied them with three other teams—the New York Giants, Arizona Cardinals, and Oakland Raiders—for worst in the National Football League.

The Chargers needed a quarterback and wanted Eli Manning, an all-American player from the University of Mississippi and the younger brother of Indianapolis Colts quarterback Peyton Manning. The problem was that Eli Manning did not want the Chargers.

A few days before the draft, Eli's father, Archie Manning—himself a former Pro Bowl quarterback—went to San Diego to talk with team officials. There were rumors that Archie did not want Eli to play for the Chargers because of what he thought was a lack of commitment to winning. Also, the rumor went, Eli could make more money from endorsements if he played for New York.

Thanks, but No Thanks

A day later, Eli Manning's agent told the Chargers that the quarterback hoped San Diego would not choose him and that he preferred New York. Chargers officials replied that they would do what they considered best for the team.

On draft day, the Chargers took Manning with the first pick but traded him to New York for the Giants' number-four pick and two future draft choices. The deal worked in both teams' favor. Manning led the Giants to a Super Bowl victory in 2008, and San Diego used its draft picks to get quarterback Philip Rivers and All-Pros Nick Kaeding and Shawn Merriman.

San Diego fans, however, remained angry that their team had been snubbed by Manning. LaDainian Tomlinson was upset, too, telling *USA Today*:

> **❝**Honestly, it kind of made me angry. To be the No. 1 pick is a privilege. To come out with, 'I don't want to play for this team,' hold on here. It sent the wrong message.**❞**

Revenge for the Chargers

Tomlinson, the Chargers, and their fans saw their chance for revenge during the 2005 season, when Manning and the Giants came to San Diego for a game. The fans booed Manning when he stepped off the team bus, booed him again during pregame warm-ups, and rocked Qualcomm Stadium with boos when he was introduced with the other starters. Tomlinson took note:

> **❝**They really gave the Giants a hard time, especially Eli. It was an electrifying event out there and it was like a playoff game.**❞**

Despite the heckling, Manning had a good game—352 yards passing and two touchdown passes. Tomlinson, however, had an even better one. He rushed for 192 yards and scored three touchdowns as the Chargers won, 45–23.

In 2004 the San Diego Chargers selected quarterback Eli Manning with the first overall pick in the NFL draft, but then immediately traded him to the New York Giants. Manning had made it clear he did not want to play in San Diego.

(Go back to page 23.) ◄◄

A History of Giving

Like LaDainian Tomlinson, many professional football players are generous with both their time and money. But then, so is the National Football League itself. Each year, NFL Charities gives tens of millions of dollars to a variety of organizations and sponsors dozens of programs to serve community needs.

Youth programs are an important part of the league's work. Some, such as the Punt, Pass & Kick competition and the Player Development programs, concentrate on the game itself. Others focus on education. The league funds Youth Education Towns in cities that host the Super Bowl, matches young players with study coaches, and gives Teacher of the Year awards.

Health programs include scholarships for students studying to become athletic trainers, support for physical fitness in schools, an after-school program focused on healthy eating, and the creation of a database on men's health.

Volunteer Work

The league strongly encourages players to do volunteer work through the NFL Tuesdays program, asking that players use what is normally a slow workday to visit schools, hospitals, and homeless shelters. In addition, one day is chosen each year for the Hometown Huddle, which calls on players, staff members, and their families to give a day of community service.

NFL Charities also seeks to promote cultural diversity by granting fellowships for minority coaches to work and learn in league training camps each summer. After the September 11, 2001, terrorist attacks on the United States, NFL Charities also created a special school curriculum, One World: Connecting Communities, Cultures, and Classrooms.

In addition, after 9/11 the NFL teamed with the Players Association to establish the NFL Disaster Relief Fund. The initial amount of $10 million went first to help relatives of those killed or injured in the attacks, along with those who took part in rescue and recovery efforts, such as police officers and firefighters. Then, when Hurricane Katrina ravaged the Gulf Coast in 2005, the fund was revived and collected more than $22 million.

A Philosophy of Giving

Commissioner Roger Goodell sums up the NFL's philosophy of giving on the league's Web site:

> **❝**The game of football is about more than making plays on the field. It is about making them off the field as well. Our commitment to fans and the communities that support us does not end when the final seconds tick off the game clock.**❞**

(Go back to page 29.) ◀◀

Another Record Breaker

All the hype and hoopla surrounding LaDainian Tomlinson's 2006 pursuit of the NFL's single-season touchdown record must have seemed very familiar to Shaun Alexander. Just a year earlier, the Seattle Seahawks' running back set the record LT was now trying to break.

Alexander's record-breaking year gained momentum midway in the season when he scored four touchdowns each in games against Arizona and Houston. But he still needed four touchdowns in the last two games to break the record of 27, set by Priest Holmes in 2002.

Alexander got three of them in the first game—the third coming on the final play. Coach Mike Holmgren had not wanted to take a chance on his star running back getting injured and had to be talked into sending him onto the field.

The next week, in a loss to Green Bay, Alexander scored on a one-yard run to establish a new record. His 73 yards rushing also gave him 1,880 for the season, tops in the NFL that year.

Like Tomlinson a season later, Alexander was named Most Valuable Player, among many other awards. His story took a downturn, however. Injuries dramatically limited his performance over the next two seasons, and he was released by Seattle in April 2008. (Go back to page 33.) ◄◄

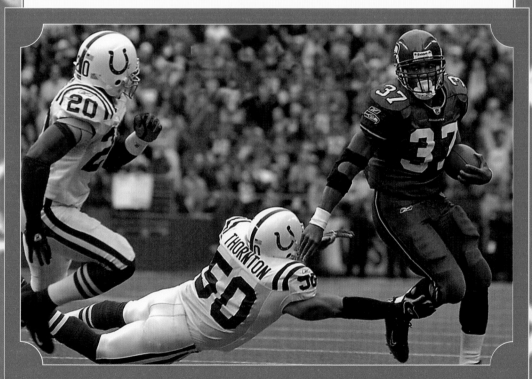

Seattle Seahawks running back Shaun Alexander slips a tackle from Indianapolis Colts linebacker David Thornton. In 2005 Alexander scored 28 touchdowns, establishing an NFL single-season record.

The Super Bowl

LaDainian Tomlinson says that his only personal goal at the start of each season is to end it by playing in the Super Bowl. Indeed, it is the dream of every NFL player to compete in the most prominent event in American sports.

The game, which annually matches the champions of the American and National Football Conferences, came about because the NFL refused to allow Lamar Hunt, a Texas billionaire, to buy a team. Angered, Hunt responded by rounding up some rich friends and creating his own league, the American Football League.

Competition between the leagues was intense, with cities such as New York, Los Angeles, and Dallas having one team from each. The rival teams battled one another for fans, media attention, and players. They tried to outbid one another for top draftees, and player salaries went up dramatically.

The Merger

With costs spiraling out of control, the two leagues decided in 1966 to merge and form two conferences—one with the old NFL teams and the other made up mostly of AFL teams. The former rivals also agreed to an annual championship game.

The championship was originally known as the AFL-NFL World Championship Game, but Hunt thought that was too long. He had been watching his children play with a highly popular toy called the Super Ball, and he suggested that perhaps *Super Bowl* would be a better fit. He really did not expect it to last, once joking:

America doesn't really stop for the Super Bowl, as the title of this 2000 book suggested. However, the game is a huge event in the United States. In 2008 some 97.5 million people—nearly one-third of the total U.S. population—watched the Super Bowl on TV.

"I was smart enough to understand that it was a corny term that would never catch on with the public.**"**

It did, of course, catch on, but not until 1969 did *Super Bowl* became the game's official name.

The Super Bowl has since become a major national event. It is one of the most watched programs on television and is the centerpiece of thousands of parties. More food is eaten on Super Bowl Sunday than on any other day except for Thanksgiving.

The game itself has frequently not lived up to expectations. Through the first 42 Super Bowls, the average winning margin has been 15 points, and in 8 games, it has been more than 25 points.

Other Attractions

Many who watch the Super Bowl, however, do so for entertainment besides football. Halftime shows have gone from marching bands to musical extravaganzas with such stars as Paul McCartney, U2, the Rolling Stones, and Michael Jackson.

Almost equally entertaining have been the Super Bowl commercials, known for their humor and creativity. The average cost of a 30-second commercial for the Super Bowl in 2008 was $2.7 million. (Go back to page 42.) ◄◄

All-Starrs

By winning the 2008 Bart Starr Award, LaDainian Tomlinson joined a list of players who have demonstrated the spirit of giving so encouraged by the National Football League. Recipients of the award, named for a Green Bay Packers Hall of Fame quarterback, have given millions of dollars and have spent countless hours helping their communities. The three players who preceded Tomlinson in winning the Bart Starr Award are good examples.

John Lynch, the Denver Broncos safety who won the award in 2007, has made it his mission to reach troubled youths through a program of positive reinforcement. He and his wife, Linda, formed the John Lynch Foundation in 2000. Its mission is to provide activities that teach teamwork, self-esteem, time management, responsibility, and determination.

In 2006 the award went to New York Jets running back Curtis Martin, who donates 10 percent of his earnings to his Job Foundation. This foundation helps a wide range of people, such as single mothers, troubled youth, recovering drug addicts, and the homeless.

The 2005 Starr Award winner was Washington Redskins safety Troy Vincent, who, like Tomlinson, won the Walter Payton Man of the Year Award. Vincent's foundation, Love Thy Neighbor, works to bring social and economic change in an effort to improve declining inner-city neighborhoods. (Go back to page 45.) ◄◄

1979 LaDainian Tomlinson is born on June 23 in Rosebud, Texas.

1996 Tomlinson rushes for 2,554 yards and scores 39 touchdowns in his senior season at Waco University High School.

1997 Tomlinson is recruited to play college football at Texas Christian University.

1999 Tomlinson sets the National Collegiate Athletic Association's major college single-game rushing record with 406 yards against the University of Texas at El Paso on November 20.

2001 Tomlinson is taken by San Diego with the fourth pick in the National Football League (NFL) draft on April 21.

Tomlinson rushes for 113 yards and scores two touchdowns on September 9 in his first NFL game.

2004 The Chargers give Tomlinson a new contract on August 13, making him the highest-paid running back in the NFL.

2005 Mckiah Renee, baby daughter of Tomlinson and his wife, LaTorsha, is stillborn on February 22.

Tomlinson scores a touchdown in his 18th straight regular-season game on October 16, tying an NFL record.

Texas Christian University celebrates "LT Day" on November 13.

2006 Tomlinson scores his 29th touchdown of the season on December 10 to set an NFL record.

2007 Tomlinson is named the NFL's Most Valuable Player on January 4. On February 23, his father, Oliver, is killed in a traffic accident in Texas.

2008 Tomlinson is forced to sit out most of the American Football Conference championship game on January 20, having suffered a knee injury the week before.

Awards and Accomplishments

1997   Texas Class 4A All-State Second Team

1998   NCAA major college rushing leader

1999   NCAA major college rushing leader, AP All-America First Team

2000   Doak Walker Running Back Award

2001   AP NFL Offensive Rookie of the Year

2002   NFL Pro Bowl selection, AP All-Pro Second Team

2003   AP All-Pro Second Team

2004   NFL Pro Bowl selection, AP All-Pro First Team

2005   NFL Pro Bowl selection

2006   NFL Pro Bowl selection, AP All-Pro First Team, *Sporting News* Sportsman of the Year, *Sports Illustrated* Best Player in the NFL, Bert Bell Award for Professional Player of the Year, Walter Payton NFL Man of the Year, NFL Rushing Leader

2007   NFL Pro Bowl selection, NFL rushing leader, ESPY Best Male Athlete Award

2008   Bart Starr Award

NFL Records

2004–05   Most consecutive games rushing for touchdowns: 18

2005–06   Most consecutive games scoring touchdowns: 18 (record co-holder)

2006   Most touchdowns, single season: 31

Most points, single season: 186

Statistics

Year	Rushing				Receiving			
	Att.	Yds.	Avg.	TDs	No.	Yds.	Avg.	TDs
2001	339	1,236	3.6	10	59	367	6.2	0
2002	372	1,683	4.5	14	79	489	6.2	1
2003	313	1,645	5.3	13	100	725	7.3	4
2004	339	1,335	3.9	17	53	441	8.3	1
2005	339	1,462	4.3	18	51	370	7.3	2
2006	348	1,815	5.2	28	56	508	9.1	3
2007	315	1,474	4.7	16	60	475	7.4	3
Totals	2,365	10,650	4.5	115	458	3,375	7.4	14

Books

Ellenport, Craig. *LaDainian Tomlinson: All-Pro on and off the Field*. Berkeley Heights, NJ: Enslow, 2006.

Freeman, Mike. *Jim Brown: The Fierce Life of an American Hero*. New York: William Morrow, 2006.

Gatto, Kimberley. *Emmitt Smith*. San Diego: Kidhaven, 2004.

Payton, Connie; Jarrett Payton; and Brittney Payton. *Payton*. New York: Rugged Land, 2005.

Polzer, Tim. *Super Bowl!* New York: DK, 2003.

Stewart, Mark. *The San Diego Chargers*. Chicago: Norwood House, 2008.

White, Reagan. *Emmitt: Running with History*. Bethesda, MD: The Calvert Group, 2002.

Web Sites

http://ladainiantomlinson.com/home.htm

LaDainian Tomlinson's official Web site includes a biography, statistics, a photo gallery, and information on Tomlinson's Touching Lives Foundation.

http://www.chargers.com

The official site of the San Diego Chargers includes information on present and past teams. The media guide includes 20 pages on LaDainian Tomlinson.

http://www.jointheteam.com/programs/programs.asp?c=6

This site gives thorough descriptions of the various programs conducted by NFL Charities.

http://www.nfl.com/history/randf

The *NFL Record and Fact Book* contains team and individual records as well as a history of the National Football League by decades.

http://www.superbowlbreakfast.com/award.aspx

This site gives the history of the Bart Starr Award, won by LaDainian Tomlinson in 2008, a biography of Starr, and descriptions of the accomplishments of past winners.

consecutive—following one after the other in order.

draft—in football, the meeting at which National Football League teams choose potential team members from among college players.

fullback—the running back whose normal position is behind the quarterback and in front of the tailback; used primarily as a blocker.

impasse—a position or situation from which there is no solution or escape; a deadlock.

interception—an instance in which a player on the opposing team catches a pass.

linebacker—a defensive player whose position is just behind the linemen; expected to help stop running plays as well as defend against passes.

option plays—plays in which the offensive player has the option of running with the ball or passing.

overtime—time added to the normal length of a game in order to break a tie; in the NFL, overtime games are won by the first team to score.

rookie—in professional sports, a player in his first year of competition.

self-centered—thinking only of oneself.

tailback—the running back whose normal position is behind the quarterback and fullback; the primary ball carrier on most teams.

upperclassman—a junior or senior in a high school or college.

wild card—in football, a playoff game in which at least one team has not won a divisional championship.

page 6 "I've had a great season . . ." *Chargers.com*, "LaDainian Tomlinson MVP Transcript." (January 4, 2007). http://www.chargers.com/news/headlines/ladainian-tomlinson-mvp.htm.

page 7 "We celebrate his season . . ." Paul Attner, "One for the Record Books." *Sporting News* (December 25, 2006). http://sportingnews.com/features/sportsman/2006/.

page 8 "LT is always coming . . ." Attner, "One for the Record Books."

page 9 "He's a legend . . ." Jim Corbett, "Tomlinson Shares Glory of Touchdown Record with Teammates." *USA Today* (December 13, 2006). http://www.usatoday.com/sports/football/nfl/chargers/2006-12-13-nfl-report_x.htm.

page 9 "I could do the party thing . . ." Attner, "One for the Record Books."

page 13 "After three turnovers . . ." Attner, "One for the Record Books."

page 14 "We were there two hours . . ." Michael Silver, "Lightning Rod." *Sports Illustrated* (September 3, 2004). http://sportsillustrated.cnn.com/2004/writers/michael_silver/09/03/silver.tomlinson/index.html.

page 19 "I kind of felt . . ." Jim Trotter, "Rookie Bounces Back Up." *San Diego Union Tribune* (September 11, 2001).

page 19 "Once they get . . ." Vinny Cerrato, "Who's More Important to the Chargers: Doug Flutie or LaDainian Tomlinson?" ESPN.com (September 30, 2001). http://scores.espn.go.com/nfl/recap?gameId=210930024.

page 20 "Never ever let someone tell you . . ." Khari Long, "Waco Native, NFL Players Give Youngsters Lessons on Football." *Baylor University Lariat* (August 5, 2003). http://www.baylor.edu/Lariat/news.php?action=story&story=18510.

page 23 "I want to be here . . ." "Chargers to Make Tomlinson Highest-Paid RB." ESPN (August 13, 2004). http://sports.espn.go.com/nfl/news/story?id=1858275.

page 25 "It was our first year . . ." K. L. Sala, "Tomlinson Rushes to Help United Way." LaDainian Tomlinson.com (June 17, 2005). http://ladainiantomlinson.com/news071505.htm.

page 27 "You really think . . ." Tom Shanahan, "LT Back to Full Strength." San Diego Hall of Champions (May 5, 2005). http://www.sdhoc.com/main/articles/chargers/LTHeal.

page 29 "We don't put a limit . . ." Sala, "Tomlinson Rushes to Help United Way."

page 30 "Every time I'm . . ." Kevin Acee, "Life in a Different Light." *San Diego Union-Tribune* (August 4, 2005). http://www.signonsandiego.com/uniontrib/20050804/news_1s4chargers.html.

page 33 "The Chargers would be wise . . ." "Chargers 2006 Player Preview." BoltTalk.com (August 11, 2006). http://bolttalk.com/?p=2632.

page 35 "When we're old . . ." "Chargers 48, Broncos 20." *USA Today* (December 10, 2006). http://www.usatoday.com/sports/scores106/106344/NFL702349.htm.

page 37 "I just told them . . ." Kate Hairopoulos, "LT Not Far from Texas Roots." *Dallas Morning News* (January 14, 2007). http://www.dallasnews.com/sharedcontent/dws/spt/football/nfl/stories/011407dnspotomlinson.32dbc38.html.

page 39 "That's vintage LT . . . " Kevin Acee, "LT Unleashed for 198 Yards, Four TDs to Finish Raiders." *San Diego Union-Tribune* (October 15, 2007). http://www.signonsandiego.com/sports/chargers/20071015-9999-1s15chargers.html.

page 40 "It's not about . . ." Michael Silver, "Waxing Poetic." Yahoo! Sports (January 4, 2008). http://sports.yahoo.com/nfl/news?slug=ms-thegameface010408&prov=yhoo&type=lgns.

page 44 "If I had kept playing . . ." Karen Crouse, "Worried About Rivers, Chargers Lose Tomlinson Instead." *New York Times* (January 21, 2008). http://www.nytimes.com/2008/01/21/sports/football/21tomlinson.html?_r=1&oref=slogin.

page 45 "She's the reason . . ." "LaDainian Tomlinson—08 Bart Starr Winner." YouTube (February 11, 2008). http://www.youtube.com/watch?v=NeA8w1NiSY4.

page 45 "My last name is Tomlinson . . . " "LaDainian Tomlinson—08 Bart Starr Winner."

page 46 "Walter Payton was the reason . . ." Tim Reynolds, "Tomlinson, Brees Share Walter Payton Man of the Year Award."

USA Today (February 2, 2007). http://www.usatoday.com/sports/football/nfl/2007-02-02-payton-award_x.htm.

page 47 "I learned [from watching Payton] . . ." Bernie Wilson, "LT Honors Payton After Passing Sweetness on Rushing TD List." *USA Today* (December 3, 2007). http://www.usatoday.com/sports/football/2007-12-03-1636558602_x.htm.

page 48 "I would have loved . . ." Jim Trotter, "Heart and Soul." *San Diego Union-Tribune* (September 9, 2004). http://www.signonsandiego.com/uniontrib/20040909/news_lz1x9ladain.html.

page 51 "Honestly, it kind of made . . ." Jarrett Bell, "Tomlinson Plays with a Mission." *USA Today* (September 1, 2004). http://www.usatoday.com/sports/football/nfl/chargers/2004-09-01-lt-mission_x.htm.

page 51 "They really gave . . ." "Eli's Career Day Drowned Out by Chargers, Fans." ESPN (September 25, 2005). http://sports.espn.go.com/nfl/recap?gameId=250925024.

page 52 "The game of football . . ." "A Message from the Commissioner." Join the Team (2005). http://www.jointheteam.com/about/commissioner.asp.

page 55 "I was smart enough . . ." "Lamar Hunt, Chiefs Owner and Sports Legend, Dies at 74." ESPN (December 14, 2006). http://sports.espn.go.com/nfl/news/story?id=2697040.

Numbers in **bold italics** refer to captions.

William W. Lace is a native of Fort Worth, Texas, where he is executive assistant to the chancellor at Tarrant County College. He holds a bachelor's degree from Texas Christian University, a master's degree from East Texas State University, and a doctorate from the University of North Texas. Prior to joining Tarrant County College, he was director of the News Service at the University of Texas at Arlington and a sportswriter and columnist for the *Fort Worth Star-Telegram*. He has written more than 45 nonfiction books for young readers on subjects ranging from the atomic bomb to the Dallas Cowboys. He and his wife, Laura, a retired school librarian, live in Arlington, Texas, and have two children and four grandchildren.

PICTURE CREDITS

page